Jane Brocket's CLEVER CONCEPTS

Cold, Crunchy, Colorful
Using Our SENSES

ROCKFORD PUBLIC LIBRARY

Millbrook Press • Minneapolis

We have five senses. With them we can

SEE, TOUCH, TASTE, SMELL, and **HEAR.**

Let's find out more about our senses.

We use our eyes to see the world around us. Tall buildings. Trees and fields.

Steep streets. Leafy paths.

Our eyes tell us about colors, patterns, and shapes.

With our eyes, we . . .
notice words and signs.
Read books.

Find numbers.

We use our ears to hear.
We can hear loud sounds:
Bells clanging. Water splashing.

Traffic honking.

And we can hear quiet sounds: Clocks ticking. Bees buzzing.

Leaves rustling.
A cat purring.

We use our hands to touch and feel.
Rough stones, smooth bricks.

Sharp spikes and a soft, fluffy flower bud.

Our feet also tell us how things feel.
If water is cold.
If grass is springy.
If socks are cozy.

How pebbles are hard and sand is grainy.

And we feel things through our skin. When the weather is cold and snowy or hot and sunny.

When it is cool and windy or wet and rainy.

We use our noses to smell.
Scented flowers.
Yeasty new bread.

Damp, earthy soil when we plant bulbs.

Some smells are nice.
Breakfast in the morning.
Blossoms in spring.
Ripe peaches in summer.

Some are stinky, like garbage or a rotten apple.

We use our tongues to taste:
Sweet candy.
Sour lemons.

Salty peanuts.
Bitter lettuce leaves.

We can taste many flavors. Juicy cherries, spicy chilies, and jammy cookies.

Oily, salty fish.
Fluffy vanilla frosting.
Cool, minty toothpaste.

Often we use more than one sense at a time. Can you say which senses we use when we . . .

cut out cookies?

Take a walk outside?

We use our five senses every day. **Can you name them all?**

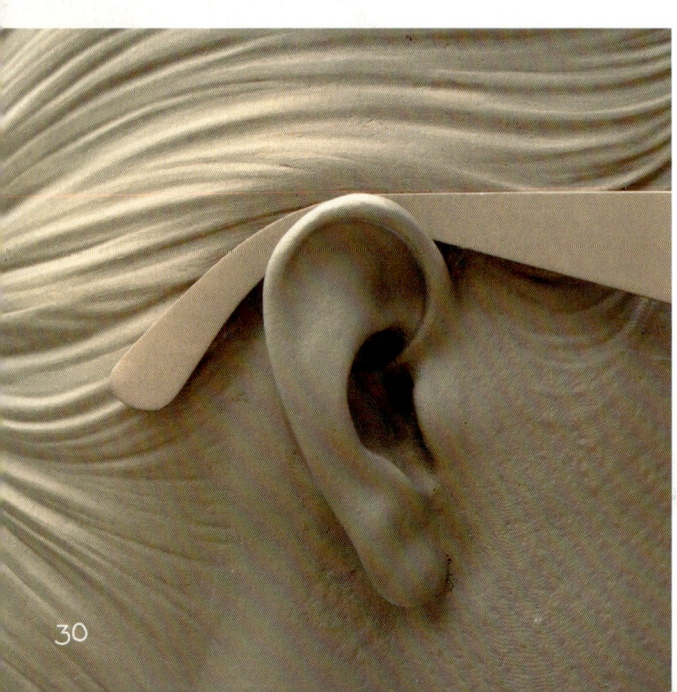

SIGHT. HEARING. TOUCH. TASTE. SMELL.

Which senses are you using now?

Text and photographs copyright © 2014 by Jane Brocket

All rights reserved. International copyright secured. No part of this book may be reproduced, stored in a retrieval system, or transmitted in any form or by any means—electronic, mechanical, photocopying, recording, or otherwise—without the prior written permission of Lerner Publishing Group, Inc., except for the inclusion of brief quotations in an acknowledged review.

Millbrook Press
A division of Lerner Publishing Group, Inc.
241 First Avenue North
Minneapolis, MN 55401 U.S.A.

For reading levels and more information, look up this title at www.lernerbooks.com.

Main body text set in Chaloops Regular 24/32.
Typeface provided by Chank.

Library of Congress Cataloging-in-Publication Data

Brocket, Jane, author.
  Cold, crunchy, colorful : Using our senses / by Jane Brocket ; photographs by Jane Brocket.
    pages   cm. — (Jane Brocket's clever concepts)
    ISBN 978–1–4677–0233–1 (lib. bdg. : alk. paper)
    ISBN 978–1–4677–2538–5 (eBook)
    1. Senses and sensation—Juvenile literature. I. Title. II. Series: Brocket, Jane. Jane Brocket's clever concepts.
  QP434.B756 2014
  612.8—dc23   2013020010

Manufactured in the United States of America
1 – BP – 12/31/13

For Tom
—J.B.

With many thanks to
Carol Hinz, Danielle Carnito,
and Anna Cavallo